Written by
Carmen S. Jones

Editor: Dorothy Ly
Cover Illustrator: Rick Grayson
Cover Designer: Rebekah O. Lewis
Production: Karen Nguyen
Art Director: Moonhee Pak
Project Director: Stacey Faulkner

Table of Contents

Introduction

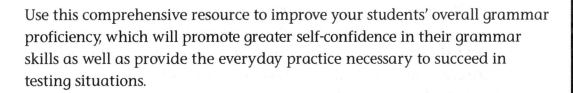

The main objective of *Grammar Minutes Grade 4* is grammar proficiency, attained by teaching students to apply grammar skills to answer questions effortlessly and rapidly. The questions in this book provide students with practice in the following key areas of fourth-grade grammar instruction:

- sentence structure
- capital letters
- nouns
- verbs
- pronouns
- adjectives
- adverbs
- subjects/predicates
- prefixes/suffixes
- abbreviations/punctuation
- prepositions

Use this comprehensive resource to improve your students' overall grammar proficiency, which will promote greater self-confidence in their grammar skills as well as provide the everyday practice necessary to succeed in testing situations.

Grammar Minutes Grade 4 features 100 "Minutes." Each Minute consists of 10 questions for students to complete within a short time period. As students are becoming familiar with the format of the Minutes, they may need more time to complete each one. Once they are comfortable and familiar with the format, give students a one- to two-minute period to complete each Minute. The quick, timed format, combined with instant feedback, makes this a challenging and motivational assignment that offers students an ongoing opportunity to improve their own proficiency in a manageable, nonthreatening way.

How to Use This Book

Grammar Minutes Grade 4 is designed to generally progress through the skills as they are introduced in the classroom in fourth grade. The Minutes can be implemented in either numerical order, starting with Minute One, or in any order based on your students' specific needs during the school year. The complexity of the sentences and the tasks within each skill being covered gradually increases so that the first Minute of a skill is generally easier than the second Minute on the same skill.

Grammar Minutes Grade 4 can be used in a variety of ways. Use one Minute a day as a warm-up activity, skill review, assessment, test prep, extra credit assignment, or homework assignment. Keep in mind that students will get the most benefit from each Minute if they receive immediate feedback. If you assign the Minute as homework, correct it in class as soon as students are settled at the beginning of the day.

If you use the Minute as a timed activity, begin by placing the paper facedown on the students' desks or displaying it as a transparency. Use a clock or kitchen timer to measure one minute—or more if needed. As the Minutes become more advanced, use your discretion on extending the time frame to several minutes if needed. Encourage students to concentrate on completing each question successfully and not to dwell on questions they cannot complete. At the end of the allotted time, have the students stop working. Read the answers from the answer key (pages 108–112) or display them on a transparency. Have students correct their own work and record their scores on the Minute Journal reproducible (page 6). Then have the class go over each question together to discuss the answers. Spend more time on questions that were clearly challenging for most of the class. Tell students that some skills that seemed difficult for them will appear again on future Minutes and that they will have another opportunity for success.

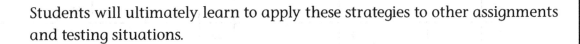

Teach students the following strategies for improving their scores, especially if you time their work on each Minute:

- leave more challenging items for last
- come back to items they are unsure of after they have completed all other items
- ask questions if they are still unsure about anything
- make educated guesses when they encounter items with which they are unfamiliar

Students will ultimately learn to apply these strategies to other assignments and testing situations.

The Minutes are designed to assess and improve grammar proficiency and should not be included as part of a student's overall language arts grade. However, the Minutes provide an excellent opportunity to identify which skills the class as a whole needs to practice or review. Use this information to plan the content of future grammar lessons. For example, if many students in the class have difficulty with a Minute on commas, additional lessons in that area will be useful and valuable for the students' future success.

While Minute scores should not be included in students' formal grades, it is important to recognize student improvements by offering individual or class rewards and incentives for scores above a certain level on a daily and/or weekly basis. Showing students recognition for their efforts provides additional motivation to succeed.

Minute Journal

Name _____

Minute	Date	Score	Minute	Date	Score	Minute	Date	Score	Minute	Date	Score
1			26			51			76		
2			27			52			77		
3			28			53			78		
4			29			54			79		
5			30			55			80		
6			31			56			81		
7			32			57			82		
8			33			58			83		
9			34			59			84		
10			35			60			85		
11			36			61			86		
12			37			62			87		
13			38			63			88		
14			39			64			89		
15			40			65			90		
16			41			66			91		
17			42			67			92		
18			43			68			93		
19			44			69			94		
20			45			70			95		
21			46			71			96		
22			47			72			97		
23			48			73			98		
24			49			74			99		
25			50			75			100		

Grammar Minutes · Grade 4 © 2009 Creative Teaching Press

Scope and Sequence

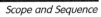

Minute 1

Name _____

Read each group of words below. If the group of words is a complete sentence, circle *Sentence*. If the group of words is not a complete sentence, circle *Fragment*.

(**Hint**: Remember that a *complete sentence* is a group of words that tells a complete thought.)

1.	Tony and Danny are going to the Tennessee Aquarium.	Sentence	Fragment
2.	Are excited about going to see the animals.	Sentence	Fragment
3.	The boys have saved their allowances to pay for the tickets.	Sentence	Fragment
4.	Danny is bringing his new digital camera.	Sentence	Fragment
5.	Tony is interested in seeing the sea otter.	Sentence	Fragment
6.	Jumps and does tricks.	Sentence	Fragment
7.	The boys have fun walking through the River Journey Exhibit.	Sentence	Fragment
8.	See reef fish and stingrays.	Sentence	Fragment
9.	Lunch at a deli across the street.	Sentence	Fragment
10.	The boys can't wait to go back with some more friends.	Sentence	Fragment

Grammar Minutes · Grade 4 © 2009 Creative Teaching Press

Minute 2

Name _____

Write the subject of each sentence on the line.
(**Hint**: The *subject* of a sentence tells who or what the sentence is about. It is usually at the beginning of a sentence.)

1. We saw flamingos on our class field trip to the zoo. _____

2. Flamingos are big pink birds with long legs. _____

3. Some people buy plastic flamingos to put on their lawn. _____

4. Kyra read that flamingos live in large groups called colonies. _____

5. The zookeeper showed us a 10-minute DVD about flamingos. _____

6. Judy was scared of them. _____

7. Our teacher tried to comfort the crying girls. _____

8. Female flamingos lay one large white egg a year. _____

9. Baby flamingos are born with gray and white feathers. _____

10. Our fourth-grade class really learned a lot about flamingos on our field trip. _____

Grammar Minutes · Grade 4 © 2009 Creative Teaching Press

Subjects

Minute 3

Name _____

Circle the predicate in each sentence.

(Hint: The predicate of a sentence tells what someone or something is or does. It is usually the last part of a sentence.)

1. Our school basketball team prepares for our first game.

2. The coach demonstrates how to dribble the ball correctly.

3. Nick blocked the ball from going into the basket.

4. John and Tim were practicing their free throws.

5. The coach showed us how to block the offense.

6. I scored a three-pointer right before the buzzer went off.

7. The cheerleaders were also practicing in the gym.

8. My sister is the captain of the cheerleading squad.

9. We run laps around the gym to strengthen our legs.

10. The team is ready for the game on Friday.

Grammar Minutes · Grade 4 © 2009 Creative Teaching Press

Minute 4

Name _____

Each of these sentences is incomplete. Circle *Subject* if the subject is missing. Circle *Predicate* if the predicate is missing.

1. The sleeping dog.   Subject   Predicate

2. Walks to the refrigerator.   Subject   Predicate

3. The woman with the pretty dress.   Subject   Predicate

4. Sasha and I.   Subject   Predicate

5. Is threading the needle to sew on a button.   Subject   Predicate

6. Are under the sink.   Subject   Predicate

7. Cried throughout the sad movie.   Subject   Predicate

8. The Girl Scouts' uniforms.   Subject   Predicate

9. Was slowly fading away.   Subject   Predicate

10. Wrinkled their noses.   Subject   Predicate

Subjects and Predicates

Minute 5

Name _____

Write the compound subject of each sentence on the line.
(Hint: A *compound subject* is made up of two or more nouns or pronouns that share the same verb in the predicate.)

1. My family and I went to Bermuda for our family vacation.

_____

2. The beaches and shops were my favorite places to visit.

_____

3. The roads and sidewalks were very narrow.

_____

4. The moon and the stars were very bright over the water.

_____

5. Dad and Kevin played golf the day before we left.

_____

6. The golf clubs and golf bag were a gift from my grandfather.

_____

7. Mom and I sent my grandparents postcards and letters before we left.

_____

8. Mom and Katie bought plenty of souvenirs for our friends

_____

9. The weather and people were very nice in Bermuda.

_____

10. Hawaii or the Grand Canyon is my choice for next year.

_____

Grammar Minutes • Grade 4 © 2009 Creative Teaching Press

Minute 6

Name _____

Circle the compound predicate in each sentence.

(**Hint**: A *compound predicate* is made up of two or more verbs that share the same subject.)

1. Bill was watching television and eating dinner.

2. Carla ran and skipped around the backyard.

3. I drew and colored the pictures.

4. The movie was created and edited in one year.

5. The storm is damaging homes and moving closer to us.

6. Mom will wash and dry my old jacket.

7. John loved the book The Indian in the Cupboard and reread it many times.

8. We are removing the collage from the wall and taking it home.

9. The runner rested and relaxed after the race.

10. Frankie yawned and stretched after her long nap.

Grammar Minutes · Grade 4 © 2009 Creative Teaching Press

Minute 7

Name _____

For Numbers 1–10, circle *Yes* if the sentence is declarative. Circle *No* if it is not.

(**Hint**: A *declarative sentence* is a statement that tells about something.)

1. Career day at our school is finally here.   Yes   No

2. Mrs. Smith, our school principal, organized the event.   Yes   No

3. A veterinarian examined a hamster right in front of us!   Yes   No

4. Mandi wanted to speak with the police officers.   Yes   No

5. Is it possible to have more than one career?   Yes   No

6. I think I want to be a nurse or a teacher.   Yes   No

7. Our teacher said she wanted to be a ballerina.   Yes   No

8. Now Mrs. Jones is happy being a teacher.   Yes   No

9. Can we go talk to the zookeeper?   Yes   No

10. Career day has helped me to decide
to become a nurse.   Yes   No

Grammar Minutes · Grade 4 © 2009 Creative Teaching Press

Minute 8

Name _____

**For Numbers 1–10, circle *Yes* if the sentence is interrogative.
Circle *No* if it is not.**

(**Hint**: An *interrogative sentence* is a question.)

1. Will we take an airplane or a train to Chicago? Yes No

2. We are going to visit my Aunt Mary and Uncle Mike. Yes No

3. Did you make sure to check the prices on a flight? Yes No

4. What day do you think we should leave? Yes No

5. How long are we going to visit them in Chicago? Yes No

6. I hope we stay for a whole week! Yes No

7. They are my favorite aunt and uncle. Yes No

8. Do you remember the time we went on a picnic? Yes No

9. Did you like Uncle Mike's grilled chicken sandwiches? Yes No

10. We can visit them for Christmas next year too. Yes No

Grammar Minutes · Grade 4 © 2009 Creative Teaching Press

Interrogative Sentences

Minute 9

Name _____

Read the sentences below. Circle *Imperative* if the sentence is imperative. Circle *Declarative* if it is declarative.
(**Hint**: An *imperative sentence* is a command. It ends with a period.)

1. Please place the apples in
   the bowl on the table.   Imperative   Declarative

2. Stop playing your music
   so loud.   Imperative   Declarative

3. We had fun at the amusement
   park last weekend.   Imperative   Declarative

4. Make sure to purchase
   the tickets for the concert.   Imperative   Declarative

5. Marlon, you need to redo your
   assignment right now.   Imperative   Declarative

6. Jonathan sells lemonade to raise
   money for summer camp.   Imperative   Declarative

7. Tell me why you are not going
   to the graduation party.   Imperative   Declarative

8. Give Justine one more chance
   to prove her point.   Imperative   Declarative

9. The doughnuts
   taste delicious.   Imperative   Declarative

10. Stop talking and
    listen to me.   Imperative   Declarative

Grammar Minutes · Grade 4 © 2009 Creative Teaching Press

Minute 10

Name _____

For Numbers 1–10, circle *Yes* if the sentence is exclamatory. Circle *No* if it is not.

(**Hint**: An *exclamatory sentence* shows strong feelings.)

1. Watch out for the deer crossing the street!   Yes   No

2. You need to slow down!   Yes   No

3. I am so glad the deer ran faster when they saw our car.   Yes   No

4. We have seen a lot of forest animals today.   Yes   No

5. Wow, that opossum ran away just in time!   Yes   No

6. Do you think we will see any more animals?   Yes   No

7. Oh, look at the eagles flying above the car!   Yes   No

8. Anna will be disappointed she didn't see the eagles.   Yes   No

9. Oh my goodness, there goes another deer!   Yes   No

10. This truly has been an amazing day!   Yes   No

Grammar Minutes · Grade 4 © 2009 Creative Teaching Press

Exclamatory Sentences

Minute 11

Name _____

For Numbers 1–3, correct the run-on sentences by adding capital letters and punctuation marks in the appropriate places to make two complete sentences.

1. The Mississippi River runs through several states we took a boat ride along the Mississippi River.

2. Clara is a talented writer she writes in her journal daily.

3. We can exchange baseball cards I have plenty you would like.

For Numbers 4–10, write *Yes* if the sentence is a run-on. Write *No* of it is not.

4. Jessica forgot to tell Tina to water her plants while she was on vacation in Boston. _____

5. The basketball player scored several baskets he is one of the best players on the team. _____

6. Sandra and Wendy have lunch on Tuesday they like to eat Italian food. _____

7. We made a rain forest float for the Thanksgiving Day Parade downtown. _____

8. Clara hopes to write novels someday. _____

9. It is nearly half past five we cannot reach town before dark. _____

10. The sun is high put on some sun block. _____

Grammar Minutes • Grade 4 © 2009 Creative Teaching Press

Minute 12

Name _____

Read each group of words below. If the group of words is a complete sentence, circle *Sentence*. If the group of words is not a complete sentence, circle *Fragment*.

1. My favorite subject.   Sentence   Fragment

2. I really enjoy art, too, because
   we make collages.   Sentence   Fragment

3. In gym class, I was the only
   one to run four laps.   Sentence   Fragment

4. Mario and Kenny.   Sentence   Fragment

5. I also like to eat lunch with
   my best friends.   Sentence   Fragment

6. After lunch we have science
   with Mrs. Moyer.   Sentence   Fragment

7. We use a microscope with
   a lot of experiments.   Sentence   Fragment

8. In math class.   Sentence   Fragment

9. In history class, we are studying
   the Gettysburg Address.   Sentence   Fragment

10. Reading the story of
    <u>Roll of Thunder, Hear My Cry.</u>   Sentence   Fragment

Grammar Minutes · Grade 4 © 2009 Creative Teaching Press

Sentence/Fragment Review

Minute 13

Name _____

Circle the subject in each sentence. Underline the predicate.

1. My mother has given my brother, my sister, and me a list of chores today.

2. She has decided that now we need more responsibilities.

3. I have to clean out the garage.

4. Maggie and Josh have to dust all of the wood furniture.

5. Josh has to trim the bushes around the porch.

6. Maggie and I will take a break after we wash the dishes.

7. Our dog Coco watches my sister and me make a snack.

8. Our father and mother have promised to take us to Pizza Place when we are done.

9. My siblings and I are excited!

10. We quickly finish all of the chores.

Grammar Minutes • Grade 4 © 2009 Creative Teaching Press

Minute 14

Name _____

For Numbers 1–5, circle the compound subject.

1. The teacher and her students are excited that the class passed the test.

2. The dog and her puppies were protected from the storm.

3. The van and the car almost collided with each other on the busy road.

4. The cereal and toast were delicious.

5. Mom and I had dinner at that restaurant.

For Numbers 6–10, add another subject.

6. Jerry and _____ both had the flu last week.

7. The cool breezes and _____ made the beach a perfect vacation spot.

8. Ed's hat and _____ blew away in the wind.

9. My hamster and _____ were my Christmas presents.

10. Joan and _____ baked oatmeal raisin cookies for their mom.

Compound Subject Review

Minute 15

Name _____

Circle the compound predicate in each sentence.

1. My brother and dad are mowing the lawn and raking the leaves.

2. Kourtney will vacuum the floors and empty the garbage.

3. Bobbi plants and waters the tulip bulbs in her garden.

4. Shawn sits and waits for his parents to pick him up from school.

5. The man thinks and wonders about his next step.

6. The singer danced around the stage and smiled at everyone.

7. My dog Duke barks and growls at the cat on the fence.

8. Martha cracks and stirs the eggs into the cake mix.

9. I spray and wipe the windows in my bedroom.

10. The little girl pouts and cries when she does not get her way.

Grammar Minutes • Grade 4 © 2009 Creative Teaching Press

Minute 16

Name _____

Read each sentence, and write the type of sentence it is on the line. Put *D* for declarative, *Int* for interrogative, *Imp* for imperative, or *E* for exclamatory.

1. Megan learned how to horseback ride this summer. _____

2. Sit up straighter on the horse. _____

3. Wow, I can't believe how fast she is going! _____

4. Can I take a picture of you and the horse? _____

5. I was so excited that Megan invited me to watch her practice! _____

6. The instructor offered to teach me as well. _____

7. I am going to ask my parents if I could take lessons. _____

8. I can't wait to learn to horseback ride! _____

9. Let's go eat lunch now. _____

10. I had so much fun spending time with Megan! _____

Types of Sentences Review

Minute 17

Name _____

For Numbers 1–3, correct the run-on sentences by adding capital letters and punctuation marks in the appropriate places to make two complete sentences.

1. The floor is wet will you dry it so no one falls?

2. We are going to the mall many stores have sales.

3. Peter will not use the car today he will take the bus to get to work.

For Numbers 4–10, write *Yes* if the sentence is a run-on. Write *No* if the sentence is not.

4. Ming is excited to travel to Japan to visit her grandmother. _____

5. She has not seen her grandmother in two years she was five years old the last time. _____

6. Ming's mother and sister will travel with her they will leave tomorrow. _____

7. Her grandmother will meet them at the airport's baggage claim. _____

8. This trip will be a nice chance for a family reunion. _____

9. Ming hopes there won't be any delays with traveling there are a few connecting fights. _____

10. It can be quite tiresome having to wait at airports because of delayed flights. _____

Minute 18

Name _____

Circle the 10 nouns in the box. Write each noun in the chart where it belongs.

veterinarian	stir	meadow	smooth	paper bag
brave	draw	souvenir	gallop	letter carrier
computer	brought	volcano	theater	creep
tennis court	gentle	dashing	preacher	pleasant

Person	Place	Thing
1. _____	4. _____	7. _____
2. _____	5. _____	8. _____
3. _____	6. _____	9. _____
		10. _____

Grammar Minutes · Grade 4 © 2009 Creative Teaching Press

Minute 19

Name _____

Circle the proper nouns in each sentence.

1. Harrison and George play baseball.

2. The name of their team is West Park Bears.

3. The boys really admire Coach Wesley.

4. He is from Jefferson City, Missouri.

5. Coach Wesley is a baseball coach for Kelly High School.

6. Each Saturday he coaches the youth baseball team.

7. The games are on Sundays in April and May.

8. Mrs. Wesley brings water and healthy snacks for the team.

9. If they win today's game, they will play against the Brownsmill Tigers.

10. The championship game will be held at Bayou Park.

Grammar Minutes · Grade 4 © 2009 Creative Teaching Press

Minute 20

Name _____

Write each noun in the box under its correct category.

building	Rocky Mountains	airport	Alaska	restaurant
Six Flags	Lake Michigan	Japan	actor	lampshade

Common Nouns	Proper Nouns
1. _____	6. _____
2. _____	7. _____
3. _____	8. _____
4. _____	9. _____
5. _____	10. _____

Grammar Minutes · Grade 4 © 2009 Creative Teaching Press

Common and Proper Nouns

Minute 21

Name _____

For Numbers 1–10, write the plural form for each noun.
(**Hint**: When a noun means more than one, it is *plural. Plural nouns* end in *–s, –es,* or *–ies.*)

1. peach   _____

2. fox   _____

3. dress   _____

4. guppy   _____

5. dish   _____

6. glass   _____

7. pineapple _____

8. branch   _____

9. toy   _____

10. country   _____

Grammar Minutes · Grade 4 © 2009 Creative Teaching Press

Minute 22

Name _____

Circle the noun that best completes each sentence.

1. Did you know that certain (animal, animals) sleep during the day?

2. An (animal, animals) that sleeps during the day and is awake at night is nocturnal.

3. My (teacher, teachers), Ms. Parker, did a lesson on nocturnal animals.

4. Kimberly and I were surprised that (skunk, skunks) are nocturnal.

5. Skunks eat insects and an occasional (rodent, rodents).

6. Skunks have long (claw, claws) that help them hunt.

7. Another nocturnal animal is a (toad, toads).

8. Toads have shorter (leg, legs) than frogs.

9. Toads hunt at night for food such as (insect, insects).

10. Next week our lesson will focus on (bat, bats).

Singular and Plural Nouns

Minute 23

Name _____

For Numbers 1–10, write the plural form for each noun.
(**Hint:** Some nouns have unusual, or *irregular*, plurals. For example, if a noun ends with −*fe*, it is often necessary to change *f* to *v* and then add −*s* to make it plural.)

1. life _____

2. tooth _____

3. goose _____

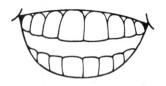

4. leaf _____

5. child _____

6. hero _____

7. person _____

8. ox _____

9. mouse _____

10. scarf _____

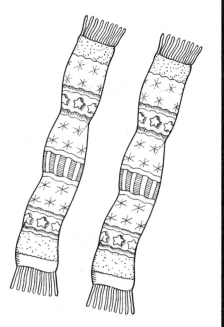

Grammar Minutes · Grade 4 © 2009 Creative Teaching Press

Minute 24

Name _____

Rewrite the underlined phrase in each sentence using a possessive noun.

1. The <u>tooth of the dog</u> was sharp.

_____

2. <u>The pencils that belonged to Riley</u> were broken.

_____

3. The <u>roof of the home</u> had leaks in ten places.

_____

4. The <u>wings of the owl</u> were one yard long when extended.

_____

5. The <u>flavor of the ice cream</u> was strawberry.

_____

6. The <u>tears on the sweater</u> came from the hanger.

_____

7. <u>The car that belonged to Luci</u> was damaged in the storm.

_____

8. The <u>remote for the television</u> needed new batteries.

_____

9. <u>The keys that belonged to Michele</u> were lost.

_____

10. <u>The burgers from In-N-Out</u> are the best.

_____

Singular Possessive Nouns

Minute 25

Name _____

Rewrite the underlined phrase in each sentence using a plural possessive noun.

1. The <u>parents of those girls</u> are famous actors.

_____

2. The <u>uniforms of the soldiers</u> were filthy.

_____

3. The <u>books the children borrowed</u> belong to the library.

_____

4. The <u>bikes of the boys</u> are red and blue.

_____

5. <u>The farm that my grandparents own</u> is located in Alabama.

_____

6. The <u>toys of the dogs</u> are old and worn out.

_____

7. The <u>faces of the models</u> were all very pretty.

_____

8. The <u>eggs of the geese</u> were very safe from predators.

_____

9. The <u>rafts of the men</u> were racing down the stream.

_____

10. The <u>prey of the wolves</u> were hiding quietly.

_____

Grammar Minutes · Grade 4 © 2009 Creative Teaching Press

Minute 26

Name _____

Use a subject pronoun from the box to replace the underlined words in each sentence. Write the pronoun on the line. (Some pronouns may be used more than once.)

(**Hint:** A *subject pronoun* takes the place of one or more nouns in the subject part of a sentence.)

you	he	she	it	we	they

1. <u>My family and I</u> will have a fantastic time on the camping trip. _____

2. <u>My parents</u> packed tents and sleeping bags into the van. _____

3. <u>My father</u> is looking forward to catching fish. _____

4. <u>My mother</u> brought pans and seasoning for cooking the fish. _____

5. <u>My brother and I</u> are putting up the tents. _____

6. <u>Shelby and Marisa</u> helped my mother clean the fish my dad caught. _____

7. <u>My piece of fish</u> was really tasty and fresh. _____

8. On Saturday <u>my family</u> went hiking on the mountain. _____

9. <u>Frank</u> almost slipped off of a rock. _____

10. I know that <u>my friends</u> will enjoy a letter about the trip. _____

Subject Pronouns

Minute 27

Name _____

For Numbers 1–5, circle the correct object pronoun to complete each sentence.
(**Hint**: An *object pronoun* takes the place of one or more nouns in the action part of a sentence.)

1. We enjoy making ice cream sundaes and eating (it, them).

2. He sits near (I, me) in class.

3. She goes with (we, us) to the movies a lot.

4. Nancy liked (she, her) very much.

5. I know (he, him) and his sister very well.

For Numbers 6–10, write an object pronoun to complete each sentence.

6. Mark liked that watch and asked me to buy _____ for his birthday.

7. I often go with both of _____ to the city to shop and do errands.

8. The puppy at the pet store had a white spot on _____.

9. Please make sure to give Robbie a hug when you see _____.

10. The water was so cool and refreshing as I drank _____.

Grammar Minutes · Grade 4 © 2009 Creative Teaching Press

Minute 28

Name _____

Circle the common nouns and underline the proper nouns in each sentence.

1. Mrs. Duncan just announced we are going to the High Museum.

2. We are going to ride the bus there next Monday.

3. Our teacher said we would see paintings from Monet.

4. My mother has a Monet painting in our family room.

5. Laci and I are excited because we also get to see ancient artifacts.

6. Unfortunately, we cannot take cameras to the museum.

7. Mrs. Jones is going to come with us.

8. After we leave the museum, we are going to have lunch at Grant Park.

9. Melody and Staci have suggested we bring blankets to sit on.

10. The boys are going to bring a football to play with after we eat.

Common and Proper Nouns Review

Minute 29

Name _____

Circle the noun that correctly completes each sentence.

1. Tonya has a teddy (bear, bears) collection.

2. She has three (bear, bears) that are ten years old.

3. Tonya's favorite bear wears reading (glass, glasses).

4. Each bear in her collection is still in the (box, boxes) that it came in.

5. Her little (sister, sisters), Jenni, has tried to take them out of the boxes.

6. Their (mother, mothers) has scolded Jenni.

7. Tonya also has a few antique (doll, dolls) as well.

8. She has a (Barbie, Barbies) from the fifties that her grandmother gave her.

9. Her grandmother also gave her a pair of antique (earring, earrings).

10. Tonya keeps them hidden in a little (case, cases) in her closet.

Grammar Minutes · Grade 4 © 2009 Creative Teaching Press

Minute 30

Name _____

For Numbers 1-6, circle the correct irregular plural noun in each group of words below.

1. loafs   loaves   loafes

2. wolfs   wolves   wolfes

3. children   childs   childrens

4. lifeies   lives   lifes

5. teethes   toothes   teeth

6. women   womans   womanes

For Numbers 7–10, write the irregular plural form for each noun.

7. cactus _____

8. sheep _____

9. knife _____

10. person _____

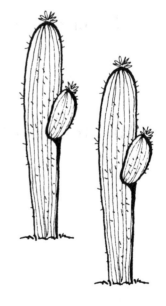

Grammar Minutes · Grade 4 © 2009 Creative Teaching Press

Irregular Plural Nouns Review

Minute 31

Name _____

For Numbers 1–10, make each phrase possessive.

1. light of the candle _____

2. uniforms of the children _____

3. pouch of the kangaroo _____

4. necklace of my mother _____

5. food of the calves _____

6. pom-poms of the cheerleaders _____

7. car of the parents _____

8. picture of the girl _____

9. teacher of the students _____

10. trumpet of the bandleader _____

Minute 32

Name _____

Rewrite the underlined phrase in each sentence using a pronoun.

1. <u>The princess</u> is wearing a beautiful dress to the ball. _____

2. She had <u>the dress</u> made by the best seamstress in the kingdom. _____

3. <u>Trina and I</u> are going to help the princess prepare for the ball. _____

4. The princess hopes to dance with <u>the prince</u>. _____

5. <u>The prince</u> is visiting from another kingdom to meet the princess. _____

6. <u>The king and queen</u> are excited for their daughter. _____

7. <u>The king</u> wants to join the two kingdoms. _____

8. The princess will ride in the carriage with <u>the king and queen</u>. _____

9. When they arrive at the ball, the prince is waiting for <u>the princess</u>. _____

10. <u>The prince</u> gives her a bouquet of roses. _____

Pronoun Review

Minute 33

Name _____

Find the verbs in the box and write them on the lines below.

pretty	destroy	lavender	breathe	slamming
sister	migrate	studio	drag	collapse
smell	mattress	dive	dentist	trample
raincoat	build	dolphin	camera	bitter

1. _____

2. _____

3. _____

4. _____

5. _____

6. _____

7. _____

8. _____

9. _____

10. _____

Grammar Minutes · Grade 4 © 2009 Creative Teaching Press

Minute 34

Name _____

Circle the verbs in each sentence.

1. Keith snores very loudly.

2. The woman sneezed after she received a big bouquet of flowers.

3. Cleo purred when Carla came into the room.

4. Bill bounces the ball on the court.

5. Susan strode her way to the finish line.

6. The fans cheered as the football star came onto the field.

7. We put our trash in the garbage can.

8. Can you see Tyra smile at the camera?

9. My dog often barks at strangers.

10. The robins are perched outside my window.

Minute 35

Name _____

Circle the correct verb tense to complete each sentence.

1. My cousin Holly now (lived, lives) in Alaska.

2. Her father once (owned, owns) a dogsled team.

3. Twice a year, the team (competes, competing) in a race.

4. This year my family is (traveling, travels) to Alaska to see them compete.

5. Holly and I (sleeping, sleep) in her room.

6. She (helps, helping) her father prepare the dogs for the race.

7. I (watch, watching) from the window because I am scared of the dogs.

8. Uncle Joseph (reassures, reassuring) me that the dogs are nice.

9. During the race, we were all (waiting, waits) for my uncle to return.

10. He (won, winning) first place this year.

Grammar Minutes · Grade 4 © 2009 Creative Teaching Press

Minute 36

Name _____

Write the past tense form of the verb in parentheses to complete each sentence.

1. Jason (kick) _____ the ball through the goalposts.

2. She (change) _____ into her costume 30 minutes ago.

3. He (bow) _____ after the audience gave him a standing ovation.

4. The magician (disappear) _____ at the end of the magic show.

5. Carrie (greet) _____ everyone at the door when they arrived.

6. The little girl (hurry) _____ to catch the bus that was driving away.

7. The prince (kneel) _____ down to kiss her hand.

8. I (measure) _____ the milk before I poured it into the cake batter.

9. We (observe) _____ the life cycle of a tadpole last month in science.

10. Terry (promise) _____ me he would do well on his exam.

Past Verb Tense

Minute 37

Name _____

For Numbers 1–10, write *Yes* if the verb is in the future tense or *No* if it is not.

1. I will perform in the ballet *The Nutcracker* next year. _____

2. Are you ordering shrimp or chicken? _____

3. I am going to scrub the kitchen floor tomorrow afternoon. _____

4. I will remember to cook the dinner tonight. _____

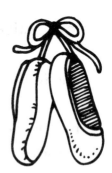

5. I will wash the clothes before I go to the game. _____

6. Stop pretending you did not hear me! _____

7. I know she will listen to you when you call her later. _____

8. I included the directions in my letter. _____

9. I will develop a plan for the science project this evening. _____

10. I had promised to clean my room when I got back. _____

Grammar Minutes · Grade 4 © 2009 Creative Teaching Press

Minute 38

Name _____

Complete the chart below by writing the correct verb form under each column.

Irregular Verb	Past Tense	Past Participle Hint: Past tense with a helping verb (*have, has, had*)
1. drive	_____	_____
2. fly	_____	_____
3. begin	_____	_____
4. ride	_____	_____
5. ring	_____	_____
6. throw	_____	_____
7. write	_____	_____
8. tell	_____	_____
9. take	_____	_____
10. shake	_____	_____

Irregular Verb Tense

Minute 39

Name _____

Write the correct form of the verb in parentheses to complete each sentence.

1. I (admit) _____ that I really like that color on the wall.

2. We (applaud) _____ when Jackson received his award.

3. Gloria is (carry) _____ the rose bouquet in the wedding.

4. Cynthia is (cheer) _____ for the Atlanta Falcons to win.

5. The baby (cry) _____ when his bottle fell to the floor.

6. I will always (disagree) _____ with her statement.

7. I will (invite) _____ Monica to the Thanksgiving dinner at our house.

8. I was (frighten) _____ when the monster jumped in front of us at the haunted house.

9. Brenda (encourage) _____ me to finish working on my science project.

10. I will (guess) _____ the answer to the last question.

Grammar Minutes · Grade 4 © 2009 Creative Teaching Press

Minute 40

Name _____

Use a linking verb from the box to complete each sentence. The words can be used more than once.

| are | seemed | is | were | am | was | feel | become | be |

1. Today will _____ my first day in fourth grade.

2. I _____ very nervous about meeting my new teacher each year.

3. Her name _____ Mrs. Robinson.

4. Mrs. Robinson _____ a second-grade teacher last year.

5. Kate and Elaine _____ excited about the first day of school.

6. They _____ up all night talking on the phone about their upcoming day.

7. When I met Mrs. Robinson today, she _____ pleasant.

8. Now I _____ better knowing that she is a nice teacher.

9. Even though she assigned homework on the first day, I _____ still excited.

10. My friends and I _____ looking forward to the rest of the school year.

Grammar Minutes • Grade 4 © 2009 Creative Teaching Press

Linking Verbs

Minute 41

Name _____

Use a helping verb from the box to best complete each sentence. The words can be used more than once.

| am | is | are | was | were | has | have | had | will |

1. The dog _____ resting his head comfortably in his owner's lap.

2. Pam _____ going to help us with the bake sale yesterday before she got sick.

3. Tom and Louie _____ solving the puzzle together when their mother called them.

4. I _____ introducing the mayor at the banquet.

5. The man _____ wandered for far too long.

6. Today we _____ travel to Florida for my sister's college graduation.

7. My grandfather and his friends _____ sharing old war stories at the reunion.

8. Jane and Eve _____ memorized their lines for the play.

9. We _____ correcting the errors we made with the experiment.

10. She _____ been sitting here in the waiting room for the doctor's appointment.

Grammar Minutes · Grade 4 © 2009 Creative Teaching Press

Minute 42

Name _____

For Numbers 1–10, write your own verb that best completes each sentence.

1. The chef is _____ a gourmet pasta dish.

2. He is _____ fish to go with the pasta.

3. We will _____ to the mall today to buy a gift for my aunt's birthday.

4. The man is _____ a place to rest after his long journey.

5. Can you _____ the key that I lost?

6. Edward will be _____ in the race tomorrow.

7. Are you _____ to the dance after the football game?

8. I will _____ my bike to the park with you.

9. The sun is _____ brighter today than it was yesterday.

10. The students are _____ clay pots in art class.

Grammar Minutes • Grade 4 © 2009 Creative Teaching Press

Verb Review

Minute 43

Name _____

Complete the chart below by writing the correct verb form under each column.

Verb	Present Participle (Hint: Continous action of a verb usually ending in -ing)	Past Participle (Hint: Completed action described by a verb usually ending with -ed)
1. receive	_____	_____
2. destroy	_____	_____
3. plan	_____	_____
4. marry	_____	_____
5. sniff	_____	_____
6. sing	_____	_____
7. swim	_____	_____
8. carry	_____	_____
9. climb	_____	_____
10. taste	_____	_____

Grammar Minutes · Grade 4 © 2009 Creative Teaching Press

Minute 44

Name _____

Circle the correct verb form to complete each sentence.

1. The baby was (awoke, awakened) by the loud noise in the middle of the night.

2. Daniel (drew, drawn) an action hero for the art contest.

3. The children (run, ran) three laps before they played tennis.

4. Diane (sweeped, swept) the kitchen floor after I washed the dishes.

5. I will (teach, taught) you how to ride a bike this summer.

6. It was (understand, understood) that he was not playing in the game.

7. The girl (weep, wept) when her parakeet suddenly flew away.

8. My mother (say, said) to come straight home after volleyball practice.

9. I (saw, seen) four movies in one month.

10. Julie had (forget, forgotten) to water the plants last week.

Irregular Verb Review

Minute 45

Name _____

Circle *Yes* if the sentence has the correct subject-verb agreement. Circle *No* if it does not. If the answer is no, write the correct verb on the line.

1. Winston has many pairs of
tennis shoes in his closet.   Yes   No _____

2. Samantha and Allison make
blueberry muffins for the bake sale.   Yes   No _____

3. The chicken sandwich tasted better
once I added barbecue sauce.   Yes   No _____

4. The thunder and lightening
scare my dog last night.   Yes   No _____

5. I hope the tomatoes grows in my
garden this year.   Yes   No _____

6. The tulips along the sidewalk
are beautiful.   Yes   No _____

7. We is going to the baseball game
to watch my brother pitch.   Yes   No _____

8. Brad fixed the broken
window yesterday.   Yes   No _____

9. Today my Uncle Fred is
arriving at the train station.   Yes   No _____

10. Ralph and Ronnie are runs
in the race today.   Yes   No _____

Minute 46

Name _____

For each sentence, write whether the underlined word is a linking verb or a helping verb.

1. Tropical rain forests <u>are</u> located in places such as Central America. _____

2. There <u>are</u> four layers of the rain forest. _____

3. The rain forest <u>is</u> usually wet because of the tropical climate. _____

4. Many animals <u>can</u> be found in the rain forest. _____

5. In class we <u>were</u> learning about the toucan and the vampire bat. _____

6. I <u>am</u> interested in knowing more about the king cobra. _____

7. The king cobra <u>is</u> located in the Southeast Asia rain forest. _____

8. The king cobra <u>is</u> brown or black. _____

9. Mrs. Crenshaw <u>has</u> promised that we will learn more about cobras. _____

10. I guess I <u>could</u> do my own research about rain forest animals. _____

Grammar Minutes • Grade 4 © 2009 Creative Teaching Press

Linking and Helping Verbs Review

Minute 47

Name _____

Circle the adjectives in the sentences below. Underline the noun that each adjective describes.

1. The bright girl did an excellent job on her project.

2. Rhonda bought four small apples from the market on Saturday.

3. Unhappy Fran decided not to go to the party.

4. The day was dreadful because of all of the storms and tornadoes.

5. The clumsy puppy fell over his huge feet as he ran.

6. The tall building is blocking my view of the park.

7. Brittany loves walking her dog in the park nearby.

8. My parents take us to the gourmet restaurant on Sundays.

9. Christian likes to eat chocolate ice cream because it tastes delicious.

10. The water in the pool is very cold.

Grammar Minutes · Grade 4 © 2009 Creative Teaching Press

Minute 48

Name _____

Complete the chart below by writing the correct form for each adjective.

Adjective	Comparative Hint: adjectives that end in "-er" compare two nouns or pronouns	Superlative Hint: adjectives that end in "-est" compare more than two nouns or pronoun
1. fast	_____	_____
2. great	_____	_____
3. soft	_____	_____
4. quick	_____	_____
5. slow	_____	_____
6. tall	_____	_____
7. low	_____	_____
8. clumsy	_____	_____
9. short	_____	_____
10. smooth	_____	_____

Grammar Minutes · Grade 4 © 2009 Creative Teaching Press

Adjectives: Comparative and Superlative

Minute 49

Name _____

Circle the adverb in each sentence. Underline the verb that the adverb describes.
(Hint: An *adverb* is a word that describes a verb and tells *how, when,* or *where* something happens.)

1. The children excitedly put on their skates at the skating rink.

2. The boys quickly dart to the rink before the girls.

3. The girls skate gracefully around the rink.

4. Mark bravely did a backwards flip in the center of the rink.

5. The children happily clapped for Mark's performance.

6. The music softly played in the background.

7. The toddlers shrieked loudly as they skated around.

8. The beginning skaters carefully stepped onto the ice.

9. Some skaters wisely wore protective gear.

10. The more experienced skaters cautiously skated around the beginners.

Grammar Minutes · Grade 4 © 2009 Creative Teaching Press

Minute 50

Name _____

For Numbers 1–10, use the adverbs in the box to best complete each sentence.

nearby	forward	usually	never	after
now	somewhere	away	forever	late

1. I look _____ to holiday shopping every year.

2. My mother and I _____ start our holiday shopping after Thanksgiving.

3. We _____ wait until the last minute when the stores are crowded.

4. This year we are going to stores that are _____.

5. _____ we are done shopping, we have lunch at my family's restaurant.

6. We plan on going _____ for our holiday vacation.

7. It seemed as if I stood in line _____ to send packages during the holidays.

8. My friends are going _____ to visit relatives for their winter vacation.

9. The heavy traffic caused us to be _____ for the New Year's party.

10. Let's make our New Year's resolutions _____.

More Adverbs

Minute 51

Name _____

For Numbers 1–6, circle the word in each sentence that begins with a prefix.

1. Before I learned how to ride a bike, I first learned how to ride a tricycle.

2. I was very unhappy when my mother said I could not go to the movies.

3. The cheerleaders used a megaphone to chant to the crowd at the game.

4. The famous singer gave me her autograph.

5. This afternoon I am going to return my library books.

6. It was impossible to finish my book last night.

For Numbers 7–10, circle the word that begins with a prefix.

7. midnight   audience   minute

8. tender   disappear   hundred

9. blackbird   preview   pitcher

10. artistic   something   nonfiction

Grammar Minutes · Grade 4 © 2009 Creative Teaching Press

Minute 52

Name _____

Add a suffix from the box to each word below. Write the new word on the line. Use each suffix only once.
(**Hint**: A *suffix* is a group of letters that changes the meaning of a word when added to the end of a word.)

> able   er   ness   ish   ion   ful   ment   est   or   ship

1. child _____

2. comfort _____

3. wonder _____

4. friend _____

5. act _____

6. govern _____

7. kind _____

8. protect _____

9. teach _____

10. smart _____

Suffiixes

Minute 53

Name _____

For Numbers 1-10, write *Yes* if the commas are in the correct place or *No* if they are not.
(**Hint:** A *comma* is a punctuation mark that is used to separate words in a list or represents a slight pause in a sentence.)

1. March 30, 2009 _____

2. San, Antonio Texas _____

3. Wednesday, April 17, 2008 _____

4. Austin Houston and Dallas, _____

5. 12561 Sycamore Lane, Atlanta, Georgia _____

6. Saturday, February 25 2010 _____

7. Sydney, Australia _____

8. pickles, lettuce, onions, tomatoes, and mayo _____

9. Boston Massachusetts, _____

10. Ken, Gabrielle Haley, John, and Julia _____

Grammar Minutes · Grade 4 © 2009 Creative Teaching Press

Minute 54

Name _____

Insert the missing commas in each sentence.

1. Judy please make sure to buy a cake for Diane's birthday.

2. Even though it had been awhile I still remembered her phone number.

3. No I do not think it will rain today.

4. Because my favorite hobby is fishing my father gave me a new fishing rod.

5. The skinny little puppy found a new home with Amy.

6. Yes I can start working on the science project next week.

7. Yasmine Karen and Lacy are going to make peanut butter and jelly sandwiches.

8. First Yasmine will take out a knife the peanut butter jelly and bread.

9. Next Karen will spread the peanut butter and jelly on the soft wheat bread.

10. Last the girls will eat their sandwiches drink milk and play board games.

Grammar Minutes · Grade 4 © 2009 Creative Teaching Press

Minute 55

Name _____

For Numbers 1–10, change the words into abbreviations whenever possible and use initials for any first and middle names. Don't forget the periods.

1. Doctor Bobby Jones _____

2. August 23 _____

3. William Christopher Handy _____

4. Second Street _____

5. Mister John Lewis Shaw _____

6. Mrs. Carol Elaine Barkley _____

7. October 12 _____

8. 1234 Marlboro Drive _____

9. Captain Douglas Harold Holmes _____

10. Atlanta, Georgia _____

Grammar Minutes · Grade 4 © 2009 Creative Teaching Press

Minute 56

Name _____

For Numbers 1–6, circle the adjectives in each sentence. Underline the nouns that the adjectives describe.

1. My beautiful mother makes the best chicken salad.

2. She uses smoked chicken that she grills on a hot fire.

3. My younger sister eats plenty of the tasty chicken salad sandwiches.

4. My older brother likes to take tiny bites to make it last longer.

5. My hardworking dad gets home too late to eat any of the delicious salad.

6. My caring mom decides to make more tasty salad for my dad.

Complete the chart below by writing the correct form for each adjective in the columns.

Adjective	Comparative (Hint: adjectives that end in "–er" compare two nouns or pronouns)	Superlative (Hint: adjectives that end in "–est" compare more than two nouns or pronouns)
7. happy	_____	_____
8. scrawny	_____	_____
9. new	_____	_____
10. tricky	_____	_____

Adjectives Review

Minute 57

Name _____

Circle the adverb in each sentence. Underline the verb that the adverb describes.

1. The students observed the caterpillars closely.

2. The baker carefully removed the bread from the oven.

3. It rains often in Seattle, Washington.

4. The plane flew high above the storm clouds.

5. I rarely travel outside of the United States.

6. I finally understood why David was upset.

7. Kylie plays the xylophone well.

8. Raymond was terribly embarrassed when he tripped over his shoelaces.

9. Karen willingly discussed the incident with the principal.

10. Today we read my favorite book by Louisa May Alcott.

Minute 58

Name _____

For Numbers 1–10, circle *prefix* if the word begins with a prefix. Circle *suffix* if the word ends with a suffix.

1. disappear   prefix   suffix

2. flawless   prefix   suffix

3. thoughtful   prefix   suffix

4. illness   prefix   suffix

5. postpone   prefix   suffix

6. development   prefix   suffix

7. protection   prefix   suffix

8. nonchalant   prefix   suffix

9. reflect   prefix   suffix

10. prehistoric   prefix   suffix

Prefixes and Suffixes Review

Minute 59

Name _____

For Numbers 1–10, write *Yes* if the commas are in the correct place or *No* if they are not.

1. Jack, Tim Danny and Toby are
on the baseball team with me.   _____

2. Kansas, City KS   _____

3. May 1, 2011   _____

4. Saturday, June 30   _____

5. Do you know the capital
of North Dakota Jasmine?   _____

6. Maria, can you please bring
me a piece of the pumpkin pie?   _____

7. My brothers play soccer,
football, baseball, and water polo.   _____

8. 12054 Sycamore Lane,
West Hills Colorado   _____

9. Wednesday
September 30 2009   _____

10. Well, you shouldn't go to the
park if you have homework to do.   _____

Grammar Minutes · Grade 4 © 2009 Creative Teaching Press

Minute 60

Name _____

Rewrite the phrases below using abbreviations and/or initials. (Don't forget the periods.)

1. also known as _____

2. Doctor Trina Jackson _____

3. September 15 _____

4. 1547 Sandy Brook Lane _____

5. United States of America _____

6. Saint Louis, Missouri _____

7. Allison Cameron Peters _____

8. Captain Hardaway _____

9. President Lincoln _____

10. December 10 _____

Abbreviations Review

Minute 61

Name _____

For Numbers 1–4, draw lines to match two words to make a compound word. Then write the word on the line.

1. light   math   _____

2. team   walk   _____

3. after   house   _____

4. cross   work   _____

For Numbers 5–10, make compound words using the words in the box below. Use each word only once.

down	fire	string	champion	ground	storm
fighter	ship	count	thunder	draw	fore

5. _____   **8.** _____

6. _____   **9.** _____

7. _____   **10.** _____

Minute 62

Name _____

For Numbers 1–10, write the two words that make up each contraction on the lines.

1. should've _____ _____

2. needn't _____ _____

3. who'll _____ _____

4. won't _____ _____

5. let's _____ _____

6. you're _____ _____

7. doesn't _____ _____

8. can't _____ _____

9. could've _____ _____

10. he'll _____ _____

Contractions

Minute 63

Name _____

Circle the synonym for each of the words in bold.

1.	**build**	apart	construct	destroy
2.	**speed**	haste	slow	shake
3.	**move**	stop	transport	invite
4.	**say**	remark	listen	watch
5.	**timid**	unafraid	shy	obey
6.	**slender**	thin	huge	nice
7.	**awkward**	easy	clumsy	awake
8.	**pain**	ache	lively	enough
9.	**mistake**	correct	right	error
10.	**depart**	early	leave	arrive

Grammar Minutes · Grade 4 © 2009 Creative Teaching Press

Minute 64

Name _____

Circle the antonym for each of the words in bold.

1. **beautiful**   attractive   ugly   pretty

2. **empty**   bare   blank   full

3. **cruel**   friendly   brutal   vicious

4. **finish**   complete   begin   done

5. **different**   opposite   same   unlike

6. **individual**   together   single   solo

7. **active**   alive   inactive   busy

8. **freeze**   withhold   solidify   melt

9. **appear**   presence   disappear   seen

10. **speechless**   talkative   quiet   silent

Antonyms

Minute 65

Name _____

Circle the correct homophones to complete each sentence.
(**Hint**: *Homophones* are words that sound the same but are spelled differently and have different meanings.)

1. Please (meat, meet) me at the (meat, meet) counter in the grocery store.

2. The (principal, principle) at my school believes in the (principal, principle) of hard work.

3. Can you (buy, by) me some ice cream at the shop (buy, by) the bookstore?

4. On (sundae, Sunday), the little girl had an ice-cream (sundae, Sunday).

5. I (knew, new) that my (knew, new) dress would be the prettiest at the ball.

6. The (rain, rein) on her horse snapped during the heavy (rain, rein).

7. The storm winds (blew, blue) the (blew, blue) spruce trees over and uprooted them.

8. The (made, maid) did her job around the house and also (made, maid) dinner.

9. My jersey ripped, (so, sew) my mom had to (so, sew) it for me before the game.

10. I checked the (whether, weather) to help me decide (whether, weather) or not to bring a jacket with me.

Grammar Minutes · Grade 4 © 2009 Creative Teaching Press

Minute 66

Name _____

For each sentence, write *Yes* if the underlined word is used correctly or *No* if it is not. If the answer is *No*, write the correct word on the second line.

1. Theodore is writing an essay <u>too</u> give to his teacher.

    _____ _____

2. We may encounter the <u>two</u> hikers in the mountains.

    _____ _____

3. I love <u>to</u> go shopping with my mother and granny.

    _____ _____

4. It is <u>too</u> hot for the children to play at the beach.

    _____ _____

5. Tim is the taller of the <u>to</u> boys.

    _____ _____

6. I can use the library <u>to</u> practice my speech for the graduation.

    _____ _____

7. Will the rain ever reach <u>to</u> the top of the hill?

    _____ _____

8. Aren't you using <u>two</u> much salt on the meat?

    _____ _____

9. Ramsey will tell us where <u>to</u> go.

    _____ _____

10. The light is <u>too</u> dim for the big ballroom.

    _____ _____

Word Usage: To, Too, Two

Minute 67

Name _____

For Numbers 1–5, write *there, their,* or *they're* to complete each sentence.

1. _____ were several places my family and I visited on our vacation to Europe.

2. My brother Kyle and sister Kay really enjoyed _____ first trip to Europe.

3. My parents were excited about going to Paris because they got married _____.

4. _____ are trains that go from country to country.

5. My parents said that _____ going to buy tickets for the train.

For Numbers 6–10, circle the correct word to complete each sentence.

6. I studied French before we left so I can speak some of it when I get (there, their, they're).

7. On the long airplane ride home, mom and Kay had to put earplugs in (there, their, they're) ears to sleep better.

8. The museum is over (there, their, they're) across the royal courtyard.

9. (There, Their, They're) so excited to see all of the popular sights!

10. (There, Their, They're) trip was very exciting and relaxing as well.

Minute 68

Name _____

For Numbers 1–10, write *Yes* if the underlined word is used correctly. Write *No* if it is not used correctly. If the answer is *No*, write the correct word on the second line.

1. The bank is closing <u>you're</u> account.   _____ _____

2. Can you please stop <u>your</u> dog from barking!   _____ _____

3. The store near <u>you're</u> home burned down.   _____ _____

4. When you go to the museum, you will see <u>your</u> favorite painting.   _____ _____

5. <u>Your</u> going to love the new restaurant by the mall!   _____ _____

6. When you see <u>your</u> father, please give him this for me.   _____ _____

7. The clock will not stop on <u>your</u> command.   _____ _____

8. <u>Your</u> going to have the time of your life at the fair.   _____ _____

9. We have to stay close to <u>you're</u> parents so we don't get lost.   _____ _____

10. Let's have <u>your</u> birthday party at the park.   _____ _____

Word Usage: Your or You're

Minute 69

Name _____

Circle *good* or *well* to complete each sentence.

1. The man in the car accident is doing (well, good).

2. Sometimes my sister doesn't listen very (well, good).

3. Because of the sunny weather, it is a (well, good) day for a picnic.

4. Kane will choose a (well, good) spot for the picnic.

5. The tears from Tiffany's eyes were not a (well, good) sign to see.

6. We will do a (well, good) job washing and cleaning out your car.

7. Rodney is out of the hospital and is doing quite (well, good).

8. Stephanie did (well, good) at her dance recital.

9. The rocky road ice cream tasted very (well, good).

10. I hope that your grandmother is doing (well, good).

Grammar Minutes · Grade 4 © 2009 Creative Teaching Press

Minute 70

Name _____

Write *affect* or *effect* to complete each sentence.
(**Hint**: *Affect* is almost always a verb; it means to influence or have an effect on. *Effect* is usually a noun; it means an outcome or result.)

1. The weather tonight may _____ whether or not we cancel the game.

2. The medicine I took for my cold had no _____ on me.

3. My allowance raise will take _____ next week.

4. After I read the book, it seemed to _____ the way I felt about the topic.

5. Rose did not let her low score on a test _____ the great mood she was in.

6. The _____ the sun had on my skin was obvious.

7. The pollution in the air can _____ people's health.

8. The illness will only _____ those who have not been vaccinated.

9. Not doing your homework will have an _____ on your grades.

10. No matter how bad situations become, it shouldn't _____ your attitude.

Grammar Minutes · Grade 4 © 2009 Creative Teaching Press

Word Usage: Affect or Effect

Minute 71

Name _____

Write *accept* or *except* to complete each sentence.
(**Hint:** *Accept* is a verb that means "to receive, admit, regard as true, or say yes." *Except* is a preposition that means "not including" or "with the exeption of.")

1. I will gladly _____ the award on your behalf since you will be out of town.

2. I like most colors _____ green and blue.

3. Jessica can do all swimming strokes _____ the butterfly.

4. Paula will _____ the apology from Cammie.

5. I can go everywhere with you today _____ for the last place.

6. All the students can go out to recess _____ Rick.

7. I can't _____ this expensive gift.

8. He bought a gift for everyone _____ me.

9. He will immediately _____ the job.

10. I am going to _____ the project even though it was late.

Minute 72

Name _____

Write a compound word to complete each sentence.

1. An insect that hops in the grass is a _____.

2. A mate that you play with is a _____.

3. A man that children
can make out of snow is a _____.

4. A bird that is black is a _____.

5. A person who fights fire is a _____.

6. A basket to put waste in is a _____.

7. A brush used to clean teeth is a _____.

8. A chair that has wheels on it is a _____.

9. A gown one would wear at night is a _____.

10. A coat used when it is raining is a _____.

Compound Words Review

Minute 73

Name _____

For Numbers 1–10, circle the correct contraction in each group.

1. I'd   i'd   Il'd

2. are't   aren't   arne't

3. the'll   they'l   they'll

4. you've   youv'e   yo've

5. woul'nd   would't   wouldn't

6. musn't   must'nt   mustn't

7. the're   they'r   they're

8. doen't   doesn't   does'nt

9. I'm   Im'   i'm

10. is'nt   isn't   is'nt

Grammar Minutes · Grade 4 © 2009 Creative Teaching Press

Minute 74

Name _____

For each set of words, write *S* if the words are *synonyms*, write *A* if the words are *antonyms*, or write *H* if the words are *homophones*.

1. every   entire   _____

2. damage   improve   _____

3. close   clothes   _____

4. destroy   create   _____

5. large   enormous   _____

6. fix   break   _____

7. better   worse   _____

8. ways   weighs   _____

9. grab   seize   _____

10. lone   loan   _____

Synonyms, Antonyms, and Homophones Review

Minute 75

Name _____

For Numbers 1–10, write *Yes* if the underlined word is used correctly. Write *No* if it is not used correctly. If the answer is *No*, write the correct word on the second line.

1. My parents like art, and <u>they're</u> favorite artist is Leonardo DaVinci.

_____ _____

2. Leonardo has <u>two</u> famous paintings that my mother loves.

_____ _____

3. <u>There</u> names are the Mona Lisa and The Last Supper.

_____ _____

4. <u>To</u> bad the originals are not for sale.

_____ _____

5. However, <u>they're</u> available as posters in museum gift shops.

_____ _____

6. I hope one day my paintings will be in <u>your</u> museum.

_____ _____

7. You have to bring <u>you're</u> passports when you travel to Europe.

_____ _____

8. The museums <u>there</u> are known for the famous artworks that are displayed.

_____ _____

9. How about we go <u>too</u> the park and have a picnic afterwards?

_____ _____

10. <u>Their</u> going to go on another trip next year.

_____ _____

Grammar Minutes · Grade 4 © 2009 Creative Teaching Press

Minute 76

Name _____

For **Numbers 1–10**, write *good* or *well* in the blank to complete each sentence.

1. Today is a _____ day to go fishing with my cousin Anthony.

2. I called him, but his mother said he was not feeling _____.

3. My Aunt Paula also didn't feel _____ that morning.

4. I was disappointed because I am not _____ at catching fish.

5. The last time we went fishing, Anthony did a _____ job of catching 10 fish.

6. I cleaned the fish _____, and our entire family had a fish fry.

7. I'm going to need a _____ night's rest after the long day.

8. I didn't sleep very _____ last night since I was so excited for the fishing trip.

9. Even though I didn't catch any fish, I had a _____ time.

10. The day was _____ worth the drive to the lake.

Word Usage Review: Good or Well

Minute 77

Name _____

For Numbers 1–10, circle the word that correctly completes each sentence.

1. With the lack of sleep, your performance will be (affected, effected).

2. The evacuation will be in (affect, effect) tonight.

3. I will have to (accept, except) the offer for help.

4. I would help you (accept, except) I'm too busy.

5. The (affect, effect) of the glare from the sun caused the car accident.

6. She finally (accepted, excepted) the fact that her lost dog is not coming home.

7. I can play most sports (accept, except) for tennis and golf.

8. The use of cell phones may (effect, affect) the brain and cause tumors.

9. Mrs. Whitley will not (accept, except) any late history projects.

10. The medicine had an immediate (effect, affect) on my headache.

Minute 78

Name _____

For Numbers 1–6, write *lose* or *loose* to complete each sentence.
(**Hint**: *Lose* is a verb that means to suffer the loss of. *Loose* is an adjective that means the opposite of tight or contained.)

1. Margo will _____ her keys if she keeps them in her big pockets.

2. A _____ wire is the reason why my car radio will not turn on.

3. I have a lot of _____ change at the bottom of my purse.

4. You are going to _____ that dog if you do not keep him on a leash.

5. Our team is going to _____ the game if we do not score one more goal.

6. My little brother has two _____ teeth on the bottom row.

For Numbers 7–10, write *Yes* if the underlined word is used correctly. Write *No* if it is not.

7. My mother has decided to eat healthy and exercise to <u>lose</u> some weight. _____

8. Her ponytail came <u>lose</u> when she ran in the all-star race. _____

9. The skirt was <u>loose</u> around my waist, but I bought it anyway. _____

10. If we do not play well in the last quarter, we will <u>lose</u> the game. _____

Word Usage: Lose or Loose

Minute 79

Name _____

Write *chose* or *choose* to complete each sentence.
(Hint: Use *chose* for past tense and *choose* for present tense.)

1. Miley _____ to stay at home instead of go to Six Flags with her friends.

2. Please hurry up and _____ the pair of jeans you are going to wear.

3. I really hope Kelly will _____ me to be on her team for the debate next week.

4. Jason _____ to fly to the graduation instead of take a train.

5. The teacher will _____ five students to be in the school play.

6. Laci _____ to have pizza last night instead of hamburgers.

7. I think I will _____ this pair of shoes because they are comfortable.

8. The dog _____ to stay outside in the rain instead of go into his doghouse.

9. I _____ the red jacket instead of the blue one.

10. I will have to _____ the best shirt to wear to my aunt's wedding.

Grammar Minutes · Grade 4 © 2009 Creative Teaching Press

Minute 80

Name _____

Write *its* or *it's* to complete each sentence.
(Hint: *Its* is the possessive form of "it." *It's* is a contraction of "it is" or "it has.")

1. The eagle soared above _____ nest in the canyon.

2. _____ not often that we go on picnics together.

3. My brother always has soccer practice, and _____ important that he is there.

4. I have ballet rehearsal four days a week, and _____ very tiring at times.

5. Today my mother is packing our lunch for the picnic and, _____ going to be delicious!

6. The cat fell asleep in _____ cozy bed.

7. _____ great to be able to spend time with family.

8. When it is hot outside, the dog naps in _____ hiding place under the porch.

9. A happy dog wags _____ tail.

10. I'm so excited because _____ almost my birthday!

Minute 81

Name _____

Write *Yes* if *than* or *then* is used correctly. Write *No* if it is not.
(Hint: *Than* is used in a sentence when comparing two things. *Then* describes a point in time.)

1. Carla likes jazz better <u>than</u> classical music.   _____

2. Simone is going to the mall and <u>then</u> the movies with Jeff.   _____

3. If you are going with us, <u>than</u> you need to hurry and get dressed.   _____

4. I prefer to scuba dive <u>than</u> surf when we go to the beach.   _____

5. Carlos would rather do his homework <u>than</u> wash dishes.   _____

6. Tony will wash his car and <u>then</u> clean out his garage.   _____

7. Leona and her mother will bake cookies and <u>than</u> cook dinner.   _____

8. Donald dances much better <u>then</u> I.   _____

9. Ken and Dan would rather go to the basketball finals <u>then</u> watch it at home.   _____

10. Florida has whiter beaches <u>than</u> South Carolina.   _____

Grammar Minutes · Grade 4 © 2009 Creative Teaching Press

Minute 82

Name _____

For Numbers 1–10, choose a word from the box to best complete each sentence. The words may be used more than once.

never	no	not	nobody
nothing	nowhere	none	neither

1. I had _____ Chicago-style pizza nor New York-style pizza.

2. We are going _____ near the Bahamas because of the hurricane.

3. I have _____ seen the new movie with my favorite actor and actress.

4. _____ will come to your party if you continue to act mean to them.

5. _____, I cannot keep giving you money to buy junk food!

6. Trisha wanted a piece of cake, but there was _____ left.

7. There was _____ in the pantry but a box of crackers and a jar of peanut butter.

8. I would _____ go skydiving out of a plane!

9. _____ of the children want to take a nap.

10. The keys were _____ to be found.

Grammar Minutes • Grade 4 © 2009 Creative Teaching Press

Word Usage: Negatives

Minute 83

Name _____

For Numbers 1–5, write *Yes* if the article is used correctly. Write *No* if it is not. If the answer is *No*, write the correct word on the second line.

1. Can we read a book Gifted Hands:
The Ben Carson Story?   _____ _____

2. An anteater walks in front of us
on our hike through the woods.   _____ _____

3. The purpose of this meeting is to
decide on the topic of our project.   _____ _____

4. The chicken salad would taste
even better if you add a apple.   _____ _____

5. Kevin found a lost dog that
everyone was looking for.   _____ _____

For Numbers 6–10, circle the correct article to complete each sentence.

6. After (an, the) game on Friday, we went for ice cream.

7. We had ice cream at (a, an) ice-cream shop by the mall.

8. I ordered vanilla ice cream with walnuts, caramel, and (the, a) cherry.

9. My sister had (a, the) banana split with lots of whipped cream.

10. I saw some of my friends at (an, the) ice-cream shop as well.

Minute 84

Name _____

Choose a preposition or prepositional phrase from the box to best complete each sentence below.

together with	about	after	instead of	in
between	by	of	beneath	into

1. Today my teacher announced we were going to read a book _____ a pig and a spider.

2. The title _____ the book is Charlotte's Web.

3. My mother and I went to the bookstore _____ school to purchase the book.

4. At first we did not see any, but luckily we found one _____ another book.

5. My mother read magazines _____ looking around the store with me.

6. I ran _____ my best friend, Katie, at the bookstore.

7. _____ Katie, I shopped for more books.

8. _____ the two of us, we bought six books to add to our collections.

9. _____ the time we were done, the store was closing.

10. My mother was already _____ line with her magazines.

Prepositions

Minute 85

Name _____

For Numbers 1–4, circle the correct word to complete each sentence.

1. You will (lose, loose) your keys if you are not careful.

2. Her shoelaces came (lose, loose) when she was running the race.

3. I will (chose, choose) my team members for the speech debate.

4. I (chose, choose) to go to the grocery store instead of the farmer's market.

For Numbers 5–10, write _lose, loose, chose,_ or _choose_ to best complete each sentence.

5. I am trying to _____ whether to play soccer or softball.

6. If you keep wearing pants with holes in the pocket, you may _____ your wallet.

7. His shoestrings were _____ during the race, causing him to trip and fall.

8. Gary _____ to stay at home instead of go to the movies.

9. Hannah did not _____ any teeth until the end of first grade.

10. Paul _____ to wash his dog this morning instead of this evening.

Grammar Minutes · Grade 4 © 2009 Creative Teaching Press

Minute 86

Name _____

For Numbers 1–5, write *than* or *then* to complete each sentence.

1. Vanessa watched the shooting star and _____ made a wish.

2. Nicole will eat lunch and _____ go shopping with her mother for new clothes.

3. I think I would rather run track _____ join the swim team this school year.

4. We broke the door hinge when we opened it farther _____ it was supposed to go.

5. The teacher is more patient with the students _____ the substitute teacher was.

For Numbers 6–10, write *its* or *it's* to complete each sentence.

6. _____ a great day to go swimming in my pool.

7. I think I will wear my pink and green swimsuit with _____ matching sun hat.

8. My mother said _____ not a good idea for me to do a flip off the diving board.

9. The diving board isn't hanging properly because _____ missing a few screws.

10. The dog licked _____ paws after it came inside.

Grammar Minutes · Grade 4 © 2009 Creative Teaching Press

Word Usage Review: Than, Then, Its, It's

Minute 87

Name _____

For Numbers 1–5, write *Yes* if the underlined words are used correctly. Write *No* if they are not.

1. I barely had <u>no</u> money left over to buy the cupcakes. _____

2. Shawn <u>doesn't</u> have invitations left to pass out for his party. _____

3. Darby could find <u>nowhere</u> to park at the grocery store. _____

4. Chris hardly has <u>no</u> experience as a firefighter. _____

5. I don't have <u>nobody</u> to watch my dog while I am out of town. _____

For Numbers 6–10, choose a word from the box to best complete each sentence.

scarcely	no one	barely	not	hardly

6. Claudia _____ had enough time to write her research paper on Miles Davis.

7. She was _____ able to find his autobiography at the bookstore.

8. Her dad could _____ afford to buy the rare jazz albums for his collection.

9. Luckily, her mother put the recordings away so _____ could break them.

10. At her presentation, Claudia _____ made a mistake and received a perfect score.

Grammar Minutes · Grade 4 © 2009 Creative Teaching Press

Minute 88

Name _____

Write the correct article (a, an) for each word.

1. _____ village

2. _____ adult

3. _____ child

4. _____ shrimp

5. _____ amateur

6. _____ estimate

7. _____ necklace

8. _____ island

9. _____ anniversary

10. _____ map

Minute 89

Name _____

Circle the correct preposition or prepositional phrase to complete each sentence.

1. (Without, Within) prior knowledge, I was still able to give an acceptance speech.

2. Darcy finally was able to stop working (on, of) her report and take a break.

3. Please put the dog (out, off) while we paint the kitchen.

4. The bear was coming (towards, toward) us on the nature trail.

5. (Because of, Close to) the rain, the ice skating rink is closed.

6. The new doughnut shop is (near, next) to the barber shop in the plaza.

7. The cookie jar is on the shelf (above, upon) the toaster.

8. My favorite book was written (by, in) Chris Van Burg.

9. I sat (next to, above) Cindi on the airplane.

10. The hawk flew high (over, beneath) the trees in the forest.

Grammar Minutes · Grade 4 © 2009 Creative Teaching Press

Minute 90

Name _____

Write what the sentence is missing on the line. Put *N* for noun, *V* for verb, *P* for preposition, or *A* for adjective.

1. Polar bears are found _____ the Arctic Ocean.

2. Male polar bears _____ around 600 to 1,000 pounds.

3. A polar bear's diet consists of seals, _____ , and kelp.

4. Their _____ fur keeps them warm in the cold temperatures.

5. Polar bears have _____ paws that help them swim well.

6. They do not hibernate like other _____ .

7. The roller coaster was a scary ride _____ the amusement park.

8. The Mississippi River is one of the _____ rivers in the United States.

9. The summer reading list will be _____ on the board.

10. His checkered _____ did not match his black pinstripe suit.

Grammar Minutes • Grade 4 © 2009 Creative Teaching Press

Apply Your Grammar Knowledge

Minute 91

Name _____

Write *Yes* if the group of words is a complete sentence. Write *No* if it is not.

1. Not going to the library tomorrow. _____

2. Will you please keep my hamsters while I am on vacation? _____

3. Timothy the ball. _____

4. Are great pets to own. _____

5. Candy is not always good to eat because it can cause cavities. _____

6. We will be moving the furniture to the new house tomorrow. _____

7. Giggled when the clown came out of the cake. _____

8. Can you help me with face painting at my sister's party? _____

9. Flying kites at the park on a sunny day. _____

10. Rebecca forgot to tell her mother about the field trip to the museum. _____

Grammar Minutes · Grade 4 © 2009 Creative Teaching Press

Minute 92

Name _____

Circle the misused word in each sentence. Write the correct word on the line.

1. After the rain, their was
a lot of mud in my backyard. _____

2. Mitch and Bill miss the
championship game last night. _____

3. I doesn't know why the
lights keep blinking off and on. _____

4. There are to apples left in
the bowl to make a fruit salad. _____

5. I like most vegetables accept
tomatoes and squash. _____

6. The storm clouds covered the
blew sky before the hurricane. _____

7. You're science fair project will
probably win first place. _____

8. Dexter seen his new dirt bike
in the garage. _____

9. Greg maid sure to study for
his American history test. _____

10. I won't to be a detective for
a secret agency when I grow up. _____

Apply Your Grammar Knowledge

Minute 93

Name _____

If the sentence has a compound subject, write *CS*. If the sentence has a compound predicate, write *CP*.

1. The tires and bell on my bicycle need to be replaced. _____

2. Sunrise and sunset are my favorite sights to watch. _____

3. My father sanded down and painted my old wooden desk. _____

4. Our tour and vacation were cut short because of the storm. _____

5. The coach instructs and guides the team during warm-ups. _____

6. Chloe ran and screamed as the dog growled at her through the fence. _____

7. Jacob and his sister caught fireflies on their camping trip. _____

8. My teacher and my parents were proud of me for making honor roll. _____

9. The boys were running and jumping in the snow on the playground. _____

10. I was smiling and laughing uncontrollably at his funny jokes. _____

Grammar Minutes • Grade 4 © 2009 Creative Teaching Press

Minute 94

Name _____

For Numbers 1–6, circle the misused word in each sentence. Write the correct word on the line.

1. Oscar did quite good on his math test considering he did not study.

_____

2. Even though the idea was a good one, its not going to work for us.

_____

3. Their is a great chance that there will be a blizzard next week.

_____

4. She flower girl dress for the wedding was pink with a satin bow.

_____

5. A elevator was stuck for two hours in the Dalton Building.

_____

6. Him father is teaching him how to play golf.

_____

For Numbers 7–10, correct each sentence with capital letters and punctuation.

7. gina bought the doughuts from smiths doughnut shop

8. We moved to charlotte, north carolina from memphis tennessee

9. May we go to stone mountain park on saturday

10. mrs brock was my favorite teacher at medlock elementary

Apply Your Grammar Knowledge

Minute 95

Name _____

For Numbers 1–4, if the group of words is a sentence, write *S*. If the group of words is a fragment write *F*.

1. My new shoes. _____

2. Mindy could not go to the circus because she has the flu. _____

3. The house on the hill. _____

4. Kept me awake last night. _____

For Numbers 5–10, circle the correct word to complete each sentence.

5. The baby will (ball, bawl) if you take his (ball, bawl) away from him.

6. The student looked at the (bored, board) with a (bored, board) look on his face.

7. We will stay (inn, in) the Lakeside (inn, in) as soon as the rest of our family arrives.

8. The brave (knight, night) rode his horse into the (knight, night).

9. The students need to (right, write) their reports (right, write) away.

10. She had to (wait, weight) for her turn to use the (wait, weight) machine at the gym.

Grammar Minutes · Grade 4 © 2009 Creative Teaching Press

Minute 96

Name _____

For Numbers 1–6, rewrite the underlined phrase in each sentence using the correct pronoun.

1. <u>Lisa and Wendy</u> were surprised when their project won first place.

_____

2. <u>Oliver and I</u> tried to be on time for the party, but we were late.

_____

3. <u>Linda</u> was not happy when she found out that her dog ran away.

_____

4. <u>Jason</u> watched in awe as the butterfly emerged from the chrysalis.

_____

5. Meg planted flowers in <u>her parents'</u> garden.

_____

6. The lion chased <u>the deer</u> into the woods.

_____

For Numbers 7–10, circle whether the sentence is *declarative, interrogative, imperative,* or *exclamatory*.

7. Stand over there, and I will take your picture.
declarative   interrogative   imperative   exclamatory

8. What would you like to have for dinner?
declarative   interrogative   imperative   exclamatory

9. We are going to the park on Memorial Day.
declarative   interrogative   imperative   exclamatory

10. I am so excited for the surprise party!
declarative   interrogative   imperative   exclamatory

Grammar Minutes · Grade 4 © 2009 Creative Teaching Press

Minute 97

Name _____

For Numbers 1–5, circle the noun form that correctly completes each sentence.

1. The hottest (desert, deserts) in the world is the Sahara.

2. The Sahara has some rivers and (stream, streams) running through it.

3. The most famous (river, rivers) is the Nile River.

4. Even though it barely rains, when it does (rain, rains), it can last for hours.

5. The desert is home to some (animals, animal), including lizards and snakes.

For Numbers 6–10, circle *linking* if the underlined word is a linking verb or circle *helping* if it is a helping verb.

6. The trip to the ocean <u>was</u> peaceful.   linking   helping

7. My baby sister <u>is</u> five years old.   linking   helping

8. The Johnsons <u>are</u> driving to their grandparents' home.   linking   helping

9. Kaci <u>was</u> sad when her dog ran away.   linking   helping

10. I <u>should</u> carry the heavy box for my sister.   linking   helping

Grammar Minutes · Grade 4 · © 2009 Creative Teaching Press

Minute 98

Name _____

Circle the correct verb form to complete each sentence.

1. The little girl (pout, pouted) when she could not have her way.

2. Please do not (snatches, snatch) that from me!

3. The dog (glaring, glared) at the cat that was hiding in the tree.

4. The soldiers will (march, marched) in the parade tomorrow.

5. The (shrieking, shriek) animal scared us on the nature trail.

6. The baby (clung, clinging) to his mother when she picked him up.

7. We were able to (dodge, dodging) the truck that swerved into our lane.

8. I (wincing, winced) when my mother cleaned the cut on my finger.

9. Mary gave a low (chuckles, chuckle) when the cartoon cat tripped.

10. Phil (hums, hummed) along with the song before he played it on his trumpet.

Apply Your Grammar Knowledge

Grammar Minutes · Grade 4 © 2009 Creative Teaching Press

Minute 99

Name _____

For Numbers 1–6, use the words in the box to make compound words. Use each word only once.

1. _____

2. _____

3. _____

4. _____

5. _____

6. _____

no	room
spot	cracker
hill	ever
how	light
ball	body
fire	side

For Numbers 7–10, write *Yes* if the underlined word is used correctly. Write *No* if it is not.

7. She <u>chose</u> to stay home instead of go on the trip to the Grand Canyon. _____

8. The speech will have an <u>effect</u> on your opinion toward the candidate. _____

9. I have to <u>accept</u> the cancellation of the car warranty. _____

10. The little girl's tooth is <u>loose</u>. _____

Grammar Minutes · Grade 4 © 2009 Creative Teaching Press

Minute 100

Name _____

For Numbers 1–5, circle *Yes* if the sentence has the correct subject-verb agreement. Circle *No* if it does not. If the answer is no, write the correct verb on the line.

1. Joey taken the bus to Dalton Mall
to buy a Christmas gift.   Yes   No   _____

2. The two singers waited impatiently
to hear who won the contest.   Yes   No   _____

3. Justin and Hazel were having fun
roller skating with their friends.   Yes   No   _____

4. Susie discuss the idea with
her parents.   Yes   No   _____

5. Gary makes homemade muffins
for my party last night.   Yes   No   _____

For Numbers 6–10, correct each sentence by adding all of the missing punctuation marks.

6. If Maggie calls tell her to come an hour earlier

7. Jackson can play the drums the tambourine the flute and the guitar

8. May we eat dinner go to the movies go bowling and perhaps play pool

9. Bianca please don't forget to put the potato salad in the cooler

10. Watch out for the fawn crossing the road

Apply Your Grammar Knowledge

Minute Answer Key

Minute 1
1. Sentence
2. Fragment
3. Sentence
4. Sentence
5. Sentence
6. Fragment
7. Sentence
8. Fragment
9. Fragment
10. Sentence

Minute 2
1. We
2. Flamingos
3. Some people
4. Kyra
5. The zookeeper
6. Judy
7. Our teacher
8. Female flamingos
9. Baby flamingos
10. Our fourth-grade class

Minute 3
1. prepares for our first game
2. demonstrates how to dribble the ball correctly
3. blocked the ball from going into the basket
4. were practicing their free throws
5. showed us how to block the offense
6. scored a three-pointer right before the buzzer went off
7. were also practicing in the gym
8. is the captain of the cheerleading squad
9. run laps around the gym to strengthen our legs
10. is ready for the game on Friday

Minute 4
1. Predicate
2. Subject
3. Predicate
4. Predicate
5. Subject
6. Subject
7. Subject
8. Predicate
9. Subject
10. Subject

Minute 5
1. My family and I
2. The beaches and shops
3. The roads and sidewalks
4. The moon and the stars
5. Dad and Kevin
6. The golf clubs and golf bag
7. Mom and I
8. Mom and Katie
9. The weather and people
10. Hawaii or the Grand Canyon

Minute 6
1. was watching television and eating dinner
2. ran and skipped around the backyard
3. drew and colored the pictures
4. was created and edited in one year
5. is damaging homes and moving closer to us
6. will wash and dry my old jacket
7. loved the book <u>The Indian in the Cupboard</u> and reread it many times
8. are removing the collage from the wall and taking it home
9. rested and relaxed after the race
10. yawned and stretched after her long nap

Minute 7
1. Yes   6. Yes
2. Yes   7. Yes
3. No   8. Yes
4. Yes   9. No
5. No   10. Yes

Minute 8
1. Yes   6. No
2. No   7. No
3. Yes   8. Yes
4. Yes   9. Yes
5. Yes   10. No

Minute 9
1. Imperative
2. Imperative
3. Declarative
4. Imperative
5. Imperative
6. Declarative
7. Imperative
8. Imperative
9. Declarative
10. Imperative

Minute 10
1. Yes   6. No
2. Yes   7. Yes
3. No   8. No
4. No   9. Yes
5. Yes   10. Yes

Minute 11
1. The Mississippi River runs through several states. We took a boat ride along the Mississippi River.
2. Clara is a very talented writer. She writes in her journal daily.
3. We can exchange baseball cards. I have plenty you would like.
4. No   8. No
5. Yes   9. Yes
6. Yes   10. Yes
7. No

Minute 12
1. Fragment
2. Sentence
3. Sentence
4. Fragment
5. Sentence
6. Sentence
7. Sentence
8. Fragment
9. Sentence
10. Fragment

Minute 13
1. subject: My mother; predicate: has given my brother, my sister, and me a list of chores today
2. subject: She; predicate: has decided that now we need more responsibilities
3. subject: I; predicate: have to clean out the garage

4. subject: Maggie and Josh; predicate: have to dust all of the wood furniture
5. subject: Josh; predicate: has to trim the bushes around the porch
6. subject: Maggie and I; predicate: will take a break after we wash the dishes
7. subject: Our dog Coco; predicate: watches my sister and me make a snack
8. subject: Our father and mother; predicate: have promised to take us to Pizza Place when we are done
9. subject: My siblings and I; predicate: are excited
10. subject: We; predicate: quickly finish all of the chores

Minute 14
1. The teacher and her students
2. The dog and her puppies
3. The van and the car
4. The cereal and toast
5. Mom and I
6–10. Answers will vary.

Minute 15
1. are mowing the lawn and raking the leaves
2. will vacuum the floors and empty the garbage
3. plants and waters the tulip bulbs in her garden
4. sits and waits for his parents to pick him up from school
5. thinks and wonders about his next step
6. danced around the stage and smiled at everyone
7. barks and growls at the cat on the fence
8. cracks and stirs the eggs into the cake mix
9. spray and wipe the windows in my bedroom
10. pouts and cries when she does not get her way

Minute Answer Key

Minute 16
1. D
2. Imp
3. E
4. Int
5. E
6. D
7. D
8. E
9. Imp
10. E

Minute 17
1. The floor is wet. Will you dry it so no one falls?
2. We are going to the mall. Many stores have sales.
3. Peter will not use the car today. He will take the bus to get to work.
4. No
5. Yes
6. Yes
7. No
8. No
9. Yes
10. No

Minute 18
1–3 Answers may be in any order.
 veterinarian
 preacher
 letter carrier
4–6 Answers may be in any order.
 tennis court
 meadow
 theater
7–10 Answers may be in any order.
 souvenir
 volcano
 computer
 paper bag

Minute 19
1. Harrison, George
2. West Park Bears
3. Coach Wesley
4. Jefferson City, Missouri
5. Coach Wesley, Kelly High School
6. Saturday
7. Sundays, April, May
8. Mrs. Wesley
9. Brownsmill Tigers
10. Bayou Park

Minute 20
1–5 Answers may be in any order.
 building
 airport
 restaurant
 lampshade
 actor
6–10 Answers may be in any order.
 Rocky Mountains
 Alaska
 Six Flags
 Japan
 Lake Michigan

Minute 21
1. peaches
2. foxes
3. dresses
4. guppies
5. dishes
6. glasses
7. pineapples
8. branches
9. toys
10. countries

Minute 22
1. animals
2. animal
3. teacher
4. skunks
5. rodent
6. claws
7. toad
8. legs
9. insects
10. bats

Minute 23
1. lives
2. teeth
3. geese
4. leaves
5. children
6. heroes
7. people
8. oxen
9. mice
10. scarves

Minute 24
1. dog's tooth
2. Riley's pencils
3. home's roof
4. owl's wings
5. ice cream's flavor
6. sweater's tears
7. Luci's car
8. television's remote
9. Michele's keys
10. In-N-Out's burgers

Minute 25
1. girls' parents
2. soldiers' uniforms
3. children's books
4. boys' bikes
5. My grandparents' farm
6. dogs' toys
7. models' faces
8. geese's eggs
9. men's rafts
10. wolves' prey

Minute 26
1. We
2. They
3. He
4. She
5. We
6. They
7. It
8. we
9. He
10. they

Minute 27
1. them
2. me
3. us
4. her
5. him
6. it
7. them
8. it
9. him
10. it

Minute 28
1. proper nouns: Mrs. Duncan, High Museum
2. common noun: bus proper noun: Monday
3. common nouns: teacher, paintings proper nouns: Monet
4. common nouns: mother, painting family room proper noun: Monet
5. common noun: artifacts proper noun: Laci
6. common nouns: cameras, museum
7. proper noun: Mrs. Jones
8. common nouns: museum, lunch proper noun: Grant Park
9. common noun: blankets proper nouns: Melody, Staci
10. common nouns: boys, football

Minute 29
1. bear
2. bears
3. glasses
4. box
5. sister
6. mother
7. dolls
8. Barbie
9. earrings
10. case

Minute 30
1. loaves
2. wolves
3. children
4. lives
5. teeth
6. women
7. cacti
8. sheep
9. knives
10. people

Minute 31
1. the candle's light
2. the children's uniforms
3. the kangaroo's pouch
4. my mother's necklace
5. the calves' food
6. the cheerleaders' pom-poms
7. the parents' car
8. the girl's picture
9. the students' teacher
10. the bandleader's trumpet

Minute 32
1. She
2. it
3. We
4. him
5. He
6. They
7. He
8. them
9. her
10. He

Minute 33
1-10 Answers may be in any order.
 smell
 destroy
 migrate
 build
 dive
 breathe
 drag
 slamming
 collapse
 trample

Minute 34
1. snores
2. sneezed, received
3. purred, came
4. bounces
5. strode
6. cheered, came
7. put
8. see, smile
9. barks
10. are perched

Minute 35
1. lives
2. owned
3. competes
4. traveling
5. sleep
6. helps
7. watch
8. reassures
9. waiting
10. won

Minute Answer Key

Minute 36
1. kicked
2. changed
3. bowed
4. disappeared
5. greeted
6. hurried
7. knelt or kneeled
8. measured
9. observed
10. promised

Minute 37
1. Yes
2. No
3. Yes
4. Yes
5. Yes
6. No
7. Yes
8. No
9. Yes
10. No

Minute 38
1. drove, driven
2. flew, flown
3. began, begun
4. rode, ridden
5. rang, rung
6. threw, thrown
7. wrote, written
8. told, told
9. took, taken
10. shook, shaken

Minute 39
1. admit
2. applauded
3. carrying
4. cheering
5. cried
6. disagree
7. invite
8. frightened
9. encouraged
10. guess

Minute 40
1. be
2. am
3. is
4. was
5. are
6. were
7. seemed or was
8. feel
9. am
10. are

Minute 41
1. is or was
2. was
3. were
4. am
5. had or has
6. will
7. were
8. have or had
9. are or were
10. has or had

Minute 42
Answers will vary.

Minute 43
1. receiving, received
2. destroying, destroyed
3. planning, planned
4. marrying, married
5. sniffing, sniffed
6. singing, sang
7. swimming, swam
8. carrying, carried
9. climbing, climbed
10. tasting, tasted

Minute 44
1. awakened
2. drew
3. ran
4. swept
5. teach
6. understood
7. wept
8. said
9. saw
10. forgotten

Minute 45
1. Yes
2. Yes
3. Yes
4. No, scared
5. No, grow
6. Yes
7. No, are
8. Yes
9. Yes
10. No, running

Minute 46
1. helping
2. linking
3. linking
4. helping
5. helping
6. helping
7. helping
8. linking
9. helping
10. helping

Minute 47
1. adjectives: bright, excellent
   nouns: girl, job
2. adjectives: four, small
   noun: apples
3. adjective: Unhappy

4. adjective: dreadful
   noun: day
5. adjectives: clumsy, huge
   nouns: puppy, feet
6. adjective: tall
   noun: building
7. adjective: nearby
   noun: park
8. adjective: gourmet
   noun: restaurant
9. adjective: delicious
   noun: chocolate
   ice cream
10. adjective: cold
    noun: water

Minute 48
1. faster, fastest
2. greater, greatest
3. softer, softest
4. quicker, quickest
5. slower, slowest
6. taller, tallest
7. lower, lowest
8. clumsier, clumsiest
9. shorter, shortest
10. smoother, smoothest

Minute 49
1. adverb: excitedly
   verb: put
2. adverb: quickly
   verb: dart
3. adverb: gracefully
   verb: skate
4. adverb: bravely
   verb: did
5. adverb: happily
   verb: clapped
6. adverb: softly
   verb: played
7. adverb: loudly
   verb: shrieked
8. adverb: carefully
   verb: stepped
9. adverb: wisely
   verb: wore
10. adverb: cautiously
    verb: skated

Minute 50
1. forward
2. usually
3. never
4. nearby
5. After
6. somewhere
7. forever
8. away
9. late
10. now

Minute 51
1. tricycle
2. unhappy
3. megaphone
4. autograph
5. return
6. impossible
7. midnight
8. disappear
9. preview
10. nonfiction

Minute 52
Possible answers.
1. childish
2. comfortable or comforter
3. wonderful
4. friendship
5. actor or action
6. government
7. kindness
8. protection, protectable, or protector
9. teacher or teachable
10. smartest, smarter, or smartness

Minute 53
1. Yes
2. No
3. Yes
4. No
5. Yes
6. No
7. Yes
8. Yes
9. No
10. No

Minute 54
1. Judy, please
2. Even though it had been awhile,
3. No, I
4. Because my favorite hobby is fishing,
5. The skinny, little
6. Yes, I
7. Yasmine, Karen, and Lacy
8. First, Yasmine will take out a knife, the peanut butter, jelly, and bread.
9. Next, Karen will spread the peanut butter and jelly on the soft wheat bread.
10. Last, the girls will eat their sandwiches, drink milk, and play board games.

Minute 55
1. Dr. B. Jones
2. Aug. 23
3. W. C. Handy
4. Second St.
5. Mr. J. L. Shaw
6. Mrs. C. E. Barkley
7. Oct. 12
8. 1234 Marlboro Dr.
9. Capt. D. H. Holmes
10. Atlanta, GA

Minute Answer Key

Minute 56
1. adjectives: beautiful, best
   nouns: mother,
   chicken salad
2. adjectives: smoked, hot
   nouns: chicken, fire
3. adjective: younger, tasty
   noun: sister chicken
   salad sandwiches
4. adjectives: older, tiny
   nouns: brother, bites
5. adjectives: hardworking,
   delicious
   nouns: dad, salad
6. adjectives: caring, tasty
   nouns: mom, salad
7. happier, happiest
8. scrawnier, scrawniest
9. newer, newest
10. trickier, trickiest

Minute 57
1. adverb: closely
   verb: observed
2. adverb: carefully
   verb: removed
3. adverb: often
   verb: rains
4. adverb: high
   verb: flew
5. adverb: rarely
   verb: travel
6. adverb: finally
   verb: understood
7. adverb: well
   verb: plays
8. adverb: terribly
   verb: embarrassed
9. adverb: willingly
   verb: discussed
10. adverb: Today
    verb: read

Minute 58
1. prefix   6. suffix
2. suffix   7. suffix
3. suffix   8. prefix
4. suffix   9. prefix
5. prefix   10. prefix

Minute 59
1. No   6. Yes
2. No   7. Yes
3. Yes   8. No
4. Yes   9. No
5. No   10. Yes

Minute 60
1. aka
2. Dr. T. Jackson
3. Sept. 15
4. 1547 Sandy Brook Ln.
5. U.S.A.

6. St. Louis, MO
7. A. C. Peters
8. Capt. Hardaway
9. Pres. Lincoln
10. Dec. 10

Minute 61
1. lighthouse
2. teamwork
3. aftermath
4. crosswalk
5–10 Answers may be in any order
   firefighter
   championship
   thunderstorm
   countdown
   drawstring
   foreground

Minute 62
1. should have
2. need not
3. who will or who shall
4. will not
5. let us
6. you are
7. does not
8. can not
9. could have
10. he will or he shall

Minute 63
1. construct
2. haste
3. transport
4. remark
5. shy
6. thin
7. clumsy
8. ache
9. error
10. leave

Minute 64
1. ugly
2. full
3. friendly
4. begin
5. same
6. together
7. inactive
8. melt
9. disappear
10. talkative

Minute 65
1. meet, meat
2. principal, principle
3. buy, by
4. Sunday, sundae
5. knew, new
6. rein, rain
7. blew, blue

8. maid, made
9. so, sew
10. weather, whether

Minute 66
1. No, to   6. Yes
2. Yes   7. Yes
3. Yes   8. No, too
4. Yes   9. Yes
5. No, two   10. Yes

Minute 67
1. There   6. there
2. their   7. their
3. there   8. there
4. There   9. They're
5. they're   10. Their

Minute 68
1. No, your
2. Yes
3. No, your
4. Yes
5. No, You're
6. Yes
7. Yes
8. No, You're
9. No, your
10. Yes

Minute 69
1. well   6. good
2. well   7. well
3. good   8. well
4. good   9. good
5. good   10. well

Minute 70
1. affect   6. effect
2. effect   7. affect
3. effect   8. affect
4. affect   9. effect
5. affect   10. affect

Minute 71
1. accept
2. except
3. except
4. accept
5. except
6. except
7. accept
8. except
9. accept
10. accept

Minute 72
1. grasshopper
2. playmate
3. snowman
4. blackbird
5. firefighter
6. wastebasket

7. toothbrush
8. wheelchair
9. nightgown
10. raincoat

Minute 73
1. I'd
2. aren't
3. they'll
4. you've
5. wouldn't
6. mustn't
7. they're
8. doesn't
9. I'm
10. isn't

Minute 74
1. S   6. A
2. A   7. A
3. H   8. H
4. A   9. S
5. S   10. H

Minute 75
1. No, their
2. Yes
3. No, Their
4. No, Too
5. Yes
6. Yes
7. No, your
8. Yes
9. No, to
10. No, They're

Minute 76
1. good   6. well
2. well   7. good
3. well   8. well
4. good   9. good
5. good   10. well

Minute 77
1. affected
2. effect
3. accept
4. except
5. effect
6. accepted
7. except
8. affect
9. accept
10. effect

Minute 78
1. lose   6. loose
2. loose   7. Yes
3. loose   8. No
4. lose   9. Yes
5. lose   10. Yes

Minute Answer Key

Minute 79
1. chose
2. choose
3. choose
4. chose
5. choose
6. chose
7. choose
8. chose
9. chose or choose
10. choose

Minute 80
1. its
2. It's
3. it's
4. it's
5. it's
6. its
7. It's
8. its
9. its
10. it's

Minute 81
1. Yes
2. Yes
3. No
4. Yes
5. Yes
6. Yes
7. No
8. No
9. No
10. Yes

Minute 82
1. neither
2. nowhere
3. not
4. Nobody
5. No
6. none
7. nothing
8. never or not
9. None
10. nowhere, not, or never

Minute 83
1. No; the
2. Yes
3. Yes
4. No; an
5. No; the
6. the
7. an
8. a
9. a
10. the

Minute 84
1. about
2. of
3. after
4. beneath
5. instead of
6. into
7. Together with
8. Between
9. By
10. in

Minute 85
1. lose
2. loose
3. choose
4. chose
5. choose
6. lose
7. loose
8. chose
9. lose
10. chose

Minute 86
1. then
2. then
3. than
4. than
5. than
6. It's
7. its
8. it's
9. it's
10. its

Minute 87
1. No
2. Yes
3. Yes
4. No
5. No
6–10 Answers may vary. Possible answers listed.
6. barely
7. not
8. scarcely
9. no one
10. hardly

Minute 88
1. a
2. an
3. a
4. a
5. an
6. an
7. a
8. an
9. an
10. a

Minute 89
1. Without
2. on
3. out
4. toward
5. Because of
6. next
7. above
8. by
9. next to
10. over

Minute 90
1. P
2. V
3. N
4. A
5. A
6. N
7. P
8. A
9. V
10. N

Minute 91
1. No
2. Yes
3. No
4. No
5. Yes
6. Yes
7. No
8. Yes
9. No
10. Yes

Minute 92
1. their, there
2. miss, missed
3. doesn't, don't
4. to, two
5. accept, except
6. blew, blue
7. You're, Your
8. seen, saw
9. maid, made
10. won't, want

Minute 93
1. CS
2. CS
3. CP
4. CS
5. CP
6. CP
7. CS
8. CS
9. CP
10. CP

Minute 94
1. good, well
2. its, it's
3. Their, There
4. She, Her
5. A, An
6. Him, His
7. Gina bought the doughnuts from Smith's Doughnut Shop.
8. We moved to Charlotte, North Carolina, from Memphis, Tennessee.
9. Can we go to Stone Mountain Park on Saturday?
10. Mrs. Brock was my favorite teacher at Medlock Elementary.

Minute 95
1. F
2. S
3. F
4. F
5. bawl, ball
6. board, bored
7. in, Inn
8. knight, night
9. write, right
10. wait, weight

Minute 96
1. They
2. We
3. She
4. He
5. their
6. it
7. imperative
8. interrogative
9. declarative
10. exclamatory

Minute 97
1. desert
2. streams
3. river
4. rain
5. animals
6. linking
7. linking
8. helping
9. linking
10. helping

Minute 98
1. pouted
2. snatch
3. glared
4. march
5. shrieking
6. clung
7. dodge
8. winced
9. chuckle
10. hummed

Minute 99
1–6 May be in any order
 ballroom,
 firecracker,
 however,
 nobody,
 hillside,
 spotlight
7. Yes
8. Yes
9. Yes
10. Yes

Minute 100
1. No, took
2. Yes
3. Yes
4. No, discussed
5. No, made
6. If Maggie calls, tell her to come an hour earlier.
7. Jackson can play the drums, the tambourine, the flute, and the guitar.
8. Can we eat dinner, go to the movies, go bowling, and perhaps play pool?
9. Bianca, please don't forget to put the potato salad in the cooler.
10. Watch out for the fawn crossing the road!